TO THE MOON

NOTEBOOK

SPACE EDITION

ARE YOU READY FOR THIS ADVENTURE ?!

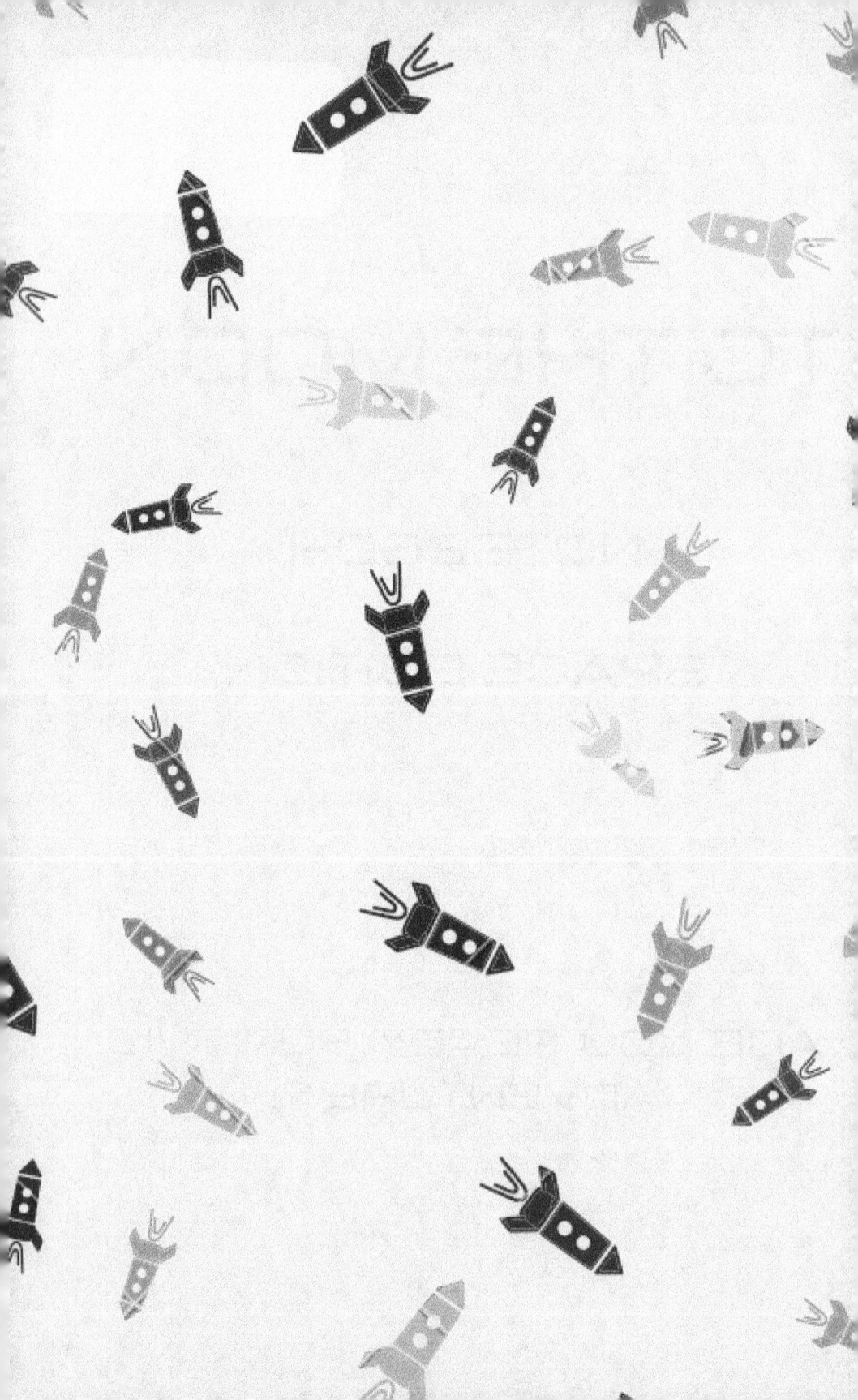

WE HOPE YOU ENJOYED IT :)

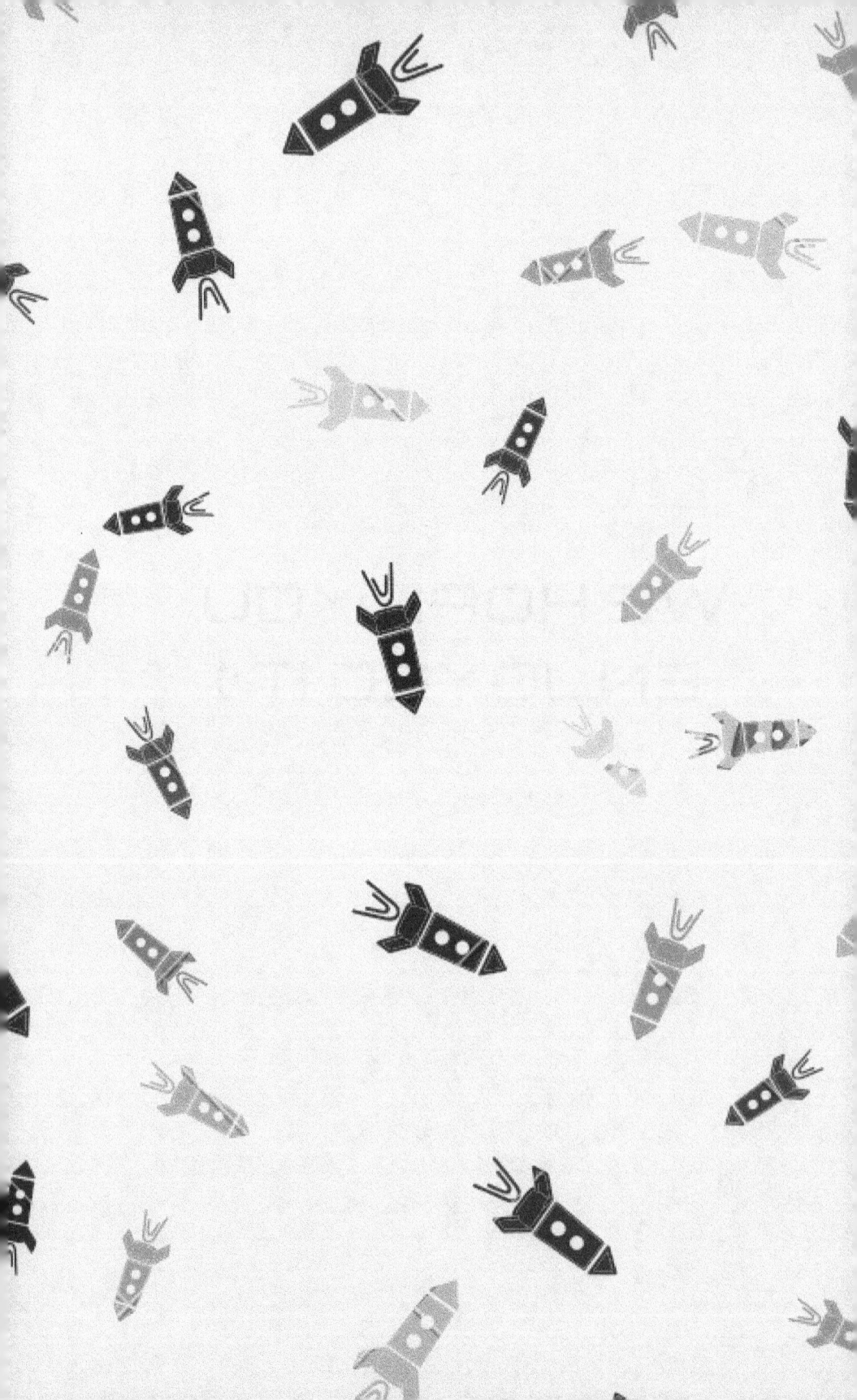

www.ingramcontent.com/pod-product-compliance
Lightning Source LLC
Chambersburg PA
CBHW071237170526
45165CB00003B/1140